The Abyss Stared Back...

A Collection of Noise Draped in a Cloak of Poetry

Preface to an Abyss

This collection is the product of exposure to trauma, a halfway decent education, a taste for using the wider scope of the English language, and a touch of misanthropy. It is best practice to go into the forthcoming lyrical hurricane with an open mind and zero expectations. The only thing that this author seeks to do is throw letters on a page for my own nefarious ends, and if the reader enjoys it, well even better.

So, I invite you, stare into the Abyss, and see if it stares back...

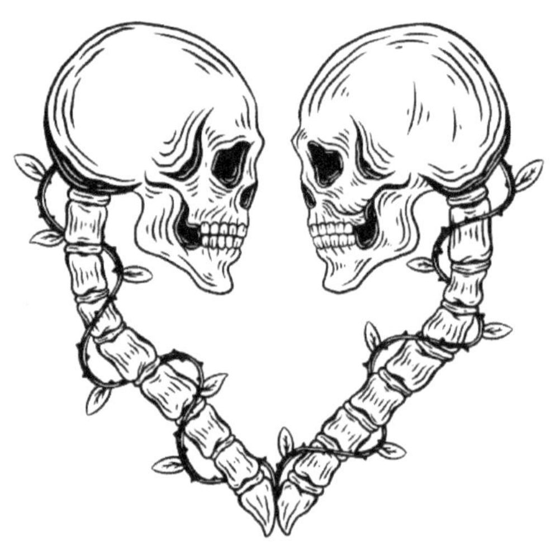

The Poppy

'midst fields of it's brethren, the Poppy grew tall,

And photosynthesised, without scourge or pall,

A simple life, lived on daylight's cue,

For the Poppy, it never knew,

Of the desperate, sunk on knees, needle in arm, spoon in hand,

All it knew was it's land, a cosmos of osmose,

And the sweet dragon of Opium it produced.

It knew not of what the hungry chase of it's sweet juice induced,

Until it's own measure of terror came to hand,

Reaping a bladed shadow across poor Poppy's land,

Roaring as tempest and thunder,

Razored edge swung low,

And rent the tall poppy asunder.

The Lady Upon The Stair

Espied a Lady upon the Stair,

Fur-coated, moonlight-scented, flame-tousled hair,

Gems at her throat, and pearls before swine,

I chanced, and asked the Lady to dine,

She scoffed, hubris-walled at such an affront,

My hat doffed, crest-falled, and heart bore the brunt,

I walked away, to watch and sigh from afar,

As the Lady, Gem-throated, Moondust coated,

Stepped from Stair to Star.

Red Rose Prose

'Twas a red Rose comprised,

Of no surprise,

Of bloom, bud, stem and thorn.

But the Rose was fooled,

When glimpsing into raindrops pooled,

viewAnd ed with naught but scorn,

For the Rose, unlike her mother,

Did not linger upon Narcissus' pool,

When She would reflect on her own aspect,

Felt only languid and cool.

But if she were to pause, and from another purview,

Another aspect would arise,

Such as that of pragmatic bees,

Who came on hands and knees,

To sup at her life-giving pollens,

Those who placed her there would stare in bold-faced wonder,

At the beauty of her growth un-sundered,

If only the Rose, would take some repose,

From painful abasement,

To adopt a new aspect, to view her lack of defect,

And wash the scorn from the thorn.

Ode to the Fur-Clad Warriors

As Thor's song rang amongst the mountains

And Skadi's grip held tight amidst the land,

The Berserkr fur-clad warriors sang their rites

Sons of Freyja, axe in hand

Fear would not waver ritual-soaked minds

For maroon-soaked blades showed purpose defined,

The fur-clad warriors could not be felled,

And howling battle-rage could not be quelled,

Kings and lords, would realise their fatal error,

At the sight of maddened butchery,

Axes in backs, flight in terror,

And Valhalla would always open it's hall door,

To any Fur-Clad finally put to the floor.

Opiate of the Masses

Religious rites are deftly proffered,

And delicious tithes are swiftly coffered,

The Lord's opiate numbs the gentle peons,

And kept them at their dealer's door for eons,

At the Crucifixes' sight: "his pain is your gain"

So their wallets continue a steady drain,

The churches gain their tax exemption,

Since the almighty dollar offers redemption,

But how far does their Lord's forgiveness stretch?

When their mouthpiece is a money-hungry lech...

From Rejection To Royalty

Great Hine-Nui wife to God-King Taane-Mahuta of the wood,

"By his side forever" thought she stood,

Till another wahine caught his wandering eye,

And to her side did the flighty god-king fly,

Hine-nui felt the deep sting of rejection and took flight

From daylight's warmth to the cold of night,

To cool the dejection that burned hot in her soul,

And seek out a new purpose,

To fill her shattered heart's hole,

That the god-king's betrayal had rent asunder,

So she travelled from a world above to the world under,

And upon a great throne of bone Hine-Nui-Te-Po would alight,

New title adopted: Great Woman of the Night,

And as Death's monarch she was the recycler of the soul,

She now had her sought purpose, she had found her role,

Some say always look up, But she had looked down,

From Rejection to Royalty, bone throne and crown.

Six Seeds

Persephone strolled, Demeter's works she admired

Hades watched, lonely and singed by desire,

And thus he reached, grasped and took her to his throne,

So that he would no longer tend the dead alone,

Demeter raged, her cold frenzy froze the land,

"Winter has come" by her now crystalline hand,

For month of six Hades had Persephone kept,

As icy tears her mother wept,

But a deal was brokered, a choice now on the table,

Whereby Persephone going forth was able,

To leave the deadlands and Hades' throne,

But for one simple caveat alone,

"You must not have tasted the food of the dead".

Six Seeds continued

With ill-ease in mind Persephone said:

"I have not, I am starved with grief and sadness",

But lo, a gardener possessed of a particular madness,

Spoke up and said: "I witnessed the eating of six pomegranate seeds",

Horror ran Persephone's face at the recounting of the deed,

But Hades loved Persephone, and couldn't bear her to suffer,

And sighed, "you are free to return to your mother"

Persephone had found love grow within her too,

"In six months, I shall return to you.

And the gardener was rewarded with a new purview,

For he was no longer just in the garden, but under it too.

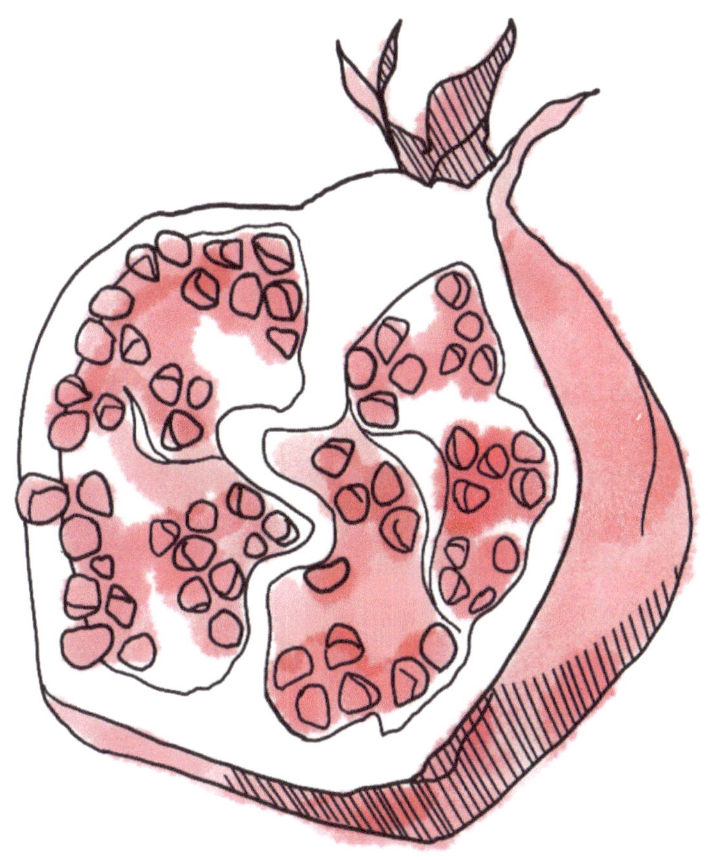

The Echo

Upon the pond where Narcissus dreamed,

There lived a nymph, perfect, it seemed,

But lo, there within lay trouble

As a fiery cauldron, her soul seemed to bubble,

For all she was cursed to voice was as she heard,

Existing as a frustrated bird,

Till love came knocking at her door,

She sought to grasp but came up sore.

So in agony, unto Death's arms did she retreat,

But a piteous gift did the gods entreat,

And offered her voice to hollow spaces and places,

And thus, unlike her, you are never alone,

for your voice forever has a clone.

Soundtrack to an illusion

A hypnotic beast with a singular diet,

Fresh dollar bills, fistfuls at a time,

The one-armed bandit with a hand clamped squarely round your wallet,

Staring you square in the eyes as it robs you blind,

All the while, singing a merry tune, telling you it's all okay,

As long as there is still cash to splash,

The illusion will hold you in neurochemical suspense,

Until reality hits like a freight train,

And it goes deadly quiet,

And you are left with little but an empty wallet,

A guilty conscience,

And a hungry beast, looking to sing it's song again

For a price...

The Bathtub

I approach, and run an apprehensive hand round the edge,

And an eager tendril rises to greet me,

The Bathtub, filled neck-deep with ichor fit for a Bathory,

Invites me to bathe in it's hungry traume,

I step in, and the maledict essence claws at my skin,

Seeking hungry purchase in a new victim,

I take a breath, and the filth chokes me,

looking for a new mouthpiece for it's vile exultations.

Finally, I am done, and prise myself free of the grasping tentacles,

The liquid suffering, thickened with the screams of the broken,

Clings to me, unwilling to release or offer me peace.

I scour myself clean, shake off the memories,

And walk away with the unsettling feeling,

That I just reached into an abyss,

And the abyss reached back...

By The Scent of a Full Blood Moon

By the scent of a full blood moon,

Accursed knights beg light to alight upon foul night,

And mourn the dawn with souls forlorn

Moon-scent brings dissent, descent, hearts rent,

From fresh-drawn blades ascent into backs turned.

In the murk of the kirk foul creatures lurk

All hungry teeth and razor claw that seek to draw,

Valuable heart-blood to mix with common mud,

But hark, are not beast and knight the same built?

Underneath fleshy scale and armour gilt?

Beats a heart eager with a fever for lifeblood,

Sadness driven to madness whets blade and claw with sprays of red

Spouts and gouts flow free all about,

By the scent of a Blood-Red Moon

A Bride Fit For A Giant

Faced with Mjölnir's arrogant theft,

Thor fell to his knees bereft,

Till brother Loki slunk to his side,

Mischievous, malicious, and swollen with pride.

"To your feet Brother, to the land of Giants we go,

Retrieve your precious Mjölnir, and lay the thieves low"

But devious thoughts lit Loki's sickly grin,

From a mind ever-hatching foul plots within,

"Hold Brother, before our course may resume

You must put on a little costume,

For today you will be a giant's bride!"

He declared, howling with laughter inside

Thor would have struck his brother clean dead for this proposition,

But it was his conniving hands that would alleviate this position,

Of his division from mighty Mjölnir

Oh so far, and yet heartbreakingly near.

A Bride Fit for a Giant Continued

So, dressed to impress in bridal dress no less,

Thor went before the Giant King as the offered bride,

As Loki watched this farce, he was dying inside,

And Mjölnir as the finest bride price

For what else would be a fitting enough prize,

For an Asgardian bride of such manly, and oddly muscularly size,

And all was well at the wedding feast,

Till Mjölnir by an enraged Thor was seized,

So gently through the air it breezed,

Until it deftly crushed the skull of the Giant Monarch,

And several others in its return arc,

The giants became aware their lifespan was to be rent asunder

As the last sound they heard,

Was the roar of mighty Mjölnir's thunder

The Lunar Sea

A baleful moon weeps upon the Lunar Sea,

An accursed sheen venting it's spleen on buccaneers adrift,

Lost marauders, freshly spat from the Phallus Sea's salty spray,

Floating now in vengeful waters where even a Dutchman would fear to Fly,

A skeleton crew whose measures of spirits have long since run dry,

Land Ho! Comes forth the echoing cry,

But No! Only a mirage in the Lunar Sea,

A falsehood with a fluid call,

Madness met with a keel haul,

What a salty crew!

The Bite of Eternal Night

As a black cloud, a bleak shroud on Europa's lands,

Sent graves descending and wringing hands,

A sick world tour carried on merchant barges,

Left inspired choirs howling aria and dirge at large,

And herbed beaks wandered streets,

Dispensing phial and fire in equal measure,

But at their feet scurried defeat,

Carrying siphonapterous gifts,

Whose succulent bite in this clouded night,

Left humanity at sanity's rift,

Drowning in failing mucosa and darkening buboes,

Finally, the kiss of waiting abyss,

The gift of the creeping bite of eternal night.

Hitting the Marks with a Wealth of Capital Punishment

A greenbacked scarlet letter,

A timeclocked harlot unfettered,

Get paid, get laid, waylaid,

By a moral compass spinning off it's axis

For what use is Heidegger's proof,

Of a theory of truth,

If none of us live any praxis?

Sell your soul to jump down the hole,

To grapple with the Bull and Bear,

Charge headfirst into the Wall,

And end up on the Street,

Trading gas, grass or ass,

Bow to the Almighty...

Nero's Student of Nietzche

Sympathy, Empathy, these things are not for you,

Staring eyes narrowed at a back-turned world

A student of Nietzche true

Raised as an object, taught no value, care for naught in turn,

And since an ice-cold world cares naught for I,

I shall play the fiddle as Rome burns

I stared into the abyss, and it stared back,

And as I pulled more daggers from my back,

My concern for others grew less and less,

Till all I saw was mess and cess,

And I ask:

"What water is there for us to clean ourselves?"

Ode to a Loner's Shadow

I am hollow within and without,

Naught but my shadow to accompany me,

Heartache wraps my soul like a crown of thorns,

Isolation burns deep, and I quench with bottles and pills,

Temporary numbness brings minor relief,

But also a shake of salt in the wound,

Sobriety reminds me once more how deep loneliness cuts,

How I ache for another,

Silent screams for no-one to hear,

Except my shadow, the constant reminder,

Of the light at the end of the tunnel.

The Painted Contract

Two faces, locked in dichotomous contract,

One, a true masterpiece, living art, breathing beauty,

The other, a Faustian nightmare,

Swollen in a lurid grin,

Flesh contorted with the essence of a life unethical,

Moral corruption by the former stains the latter,

As Mr Gray lived out his hedonism in glorious excess,

His framed shadow carried the weight of his shattered soul,

A hardened maledict glare through abyssal eyes,

A leering, black-toothed rictus,

Skin swollen, filled with Mr Gray's immoral cess,

The frame full to bursting with his shameless acts,

And as his shadow grows in exquisite horror,

Dorian lived his horrific paradise without price,

So long as his shadow was safe,

A hidden contract,

Testament to the depths humanity will reach,

If the leash is long enough.

The Lover's Fortress

I put a spell on you,

Because, you're mine

Have you strung out in a gibbet,

Over the seething moat of our love most malign,

As you peer through bars at the moon above,

Hoping to hear the aria of our fecund love,

Only the siren song of lunacy rings clear,

And the dirge of mournful wolves at your ear,

So all that is left is to stare at the walls I built and wax lyrical,

For nought I said of our love is truth,

It is purely satirical,

Till I finally pull you in close,

Whisper sweet nothings,

Bathe you in a gentle lie,

Then kindly wrap my liar's tongue around your neck,

And hang you out to dry...

From Pride to Extreme Prejudice

The scourging angel at His righteous side,

But Yahweh's hubris he could not abide,

For the angel had an ego of his own,

And from the Master's coop had flown,

Taking half of his Lord's flock,

Shattering the dream as a glass house to a rock,

Brother took blade unto brother, at Yahweh's command,

Pride in hand, blood on the sand,

The Scourge's army he hosted, boasted,

But once all was done, each face was defaced and effaced,

From the host of the firmament,

Instead cast down to a home more permanent,

Where the Scourge waits, and contemplates,

A nice Eve to pick some fruit...